SWANSEA LIBRARIES

Ymllwyd yn ôl

Withdrawn

D1614439

P.E.G

"GOOD THINGS"

SIDEBOARDS -
SETTEES and
EASY CHAIRS
CABINETS -
BEDROOM
SUITES

GANES

...LEUMS -
Soft FURNISH-
ING FABRICS

- 38 and 41 -
Queen Street

W. H. BISHOP & SON

PLUMBERS & DOMESTIC
ENGINEERS, DECORATORS
BUILDERS & CONTRACTORS
REPAIRERS

ESTABLISHED 1878

TELEPHONE 4350

THE TUDOR STEAM LAUNDRY

COMPANY

High-class Work of every
description,

Hotel and Restaurant
Work a speciality.

Head Office and Works—

30, Tudor Lane,
CARDIFF

MONDAY - SEPT. 10th

and during the week

8.0   ONCE NIGHTLY   8.0

Violet Farebrother

IN GILBERT PORTEOUS'
PRODUCTION—

THE HAPPY ENDING

A Comedy in Three Acts, by Ian Hay.

Direct from the St. James' Theatre, London

WIRELESS

Buy direct from the Manufacturer
Broadcast Crystal Receiver, £1 : 7 : 6
Approved by H.M. Postmaster General,
Stamped B.B.C. Registered No. 506
.001 Condensers - - 10/6 each
Wound Inductance Tubes,
from 2/9 each
The Largest Stock of Wireless Parts in the
Provinces

Robins Electrical & Wireless
Depot & Institute, Limited,

Retail Depot - PARK PLACE
Wholesale and Registered Offices—
85 QUEEN STREET.
Works & Stores, FANNY STREET, CATHAYS

Telephone 5176

GOUGH'S DELIGHTFUL CHAR-A-BANCS

Smartest
and Best

THE FINEST
AND
LARGEST FLEET
IN WALES
—o—
Try Them   Low Rates

GOUGH'S GARAGE CO.

Hodges Row, CARDIFF.   Phone 3993.   And at
61 Foreland Rd., WHITCHURCH, „ 187. Mountain Ash

STEWART WILLIAMS'
CARDIFF
YESTERDAY
No.10

1 (*overleaf*) Thousands throng Queen Street to welcome home the Welsh Volunteer Detachment
on their return from the South African War in 1902

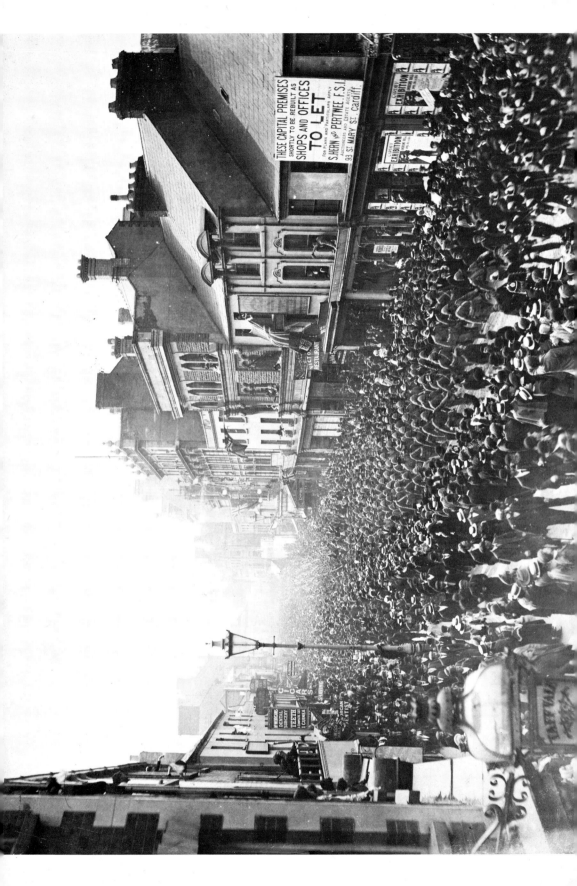

STEWART WILLIAMS'
CARDIFF
YESTERDAY
No.10

WEST GLAMORGAN COUNTY LIBRARIES

Introduction by
Geoff Dart

First Published November, 1984

© Stewart Williams, Publishers,
1 Trem-y-Don, Barry,
South Glamorgan

ISBN 0 900807 63 6

WEST GLAMORGAN COUNTY LIBRARY

651001   £6.95

DECEMBER 1984

CLASS NO N42 98708102 2 2
W.H. 4·91
LOCATION 87

Our since   heir
photogra

Llewellyn   L.
Bear (120,   C.
Bridger (1   , Lionel Clode (46, 48, 60,
61); H. O.   , 195, 196, 197); Stan Coleman (150); M. Comrie (118, 119); S. G.
Davies (62, 63, 136, 137); Shirley and Reg Dobbins (213); Brian Duddridge (75); W. Durham (73);
Lionel V. Evans (87, 210); Stan Fenton (168, 169, 170, 171, 172, 173); Mrs Clarice Good (191); G.
Green (146); Glyn Griffiths (64); John Griffiths (91, 205); Sid Grimshaw (192); Ken Hollyman
(138, 139, 142); Mrs P. Howells (162); Tommy Hutchinson (177); J. Iles (96); G. James (94, 95,
204); Mrs Ann R. Jones (198, 199, 200, 201); Fred Jones (4, 7, 8, 17, 18, 19, 20, 21, 23, 24, 25, 26,
27, 28, 31, 32, 37, 38, 39, 40, 47 52, 53, 56, 57, 67, 68, 84, 85, 86, 90, 92, 132, 156, 166, 193, 194,
203); Alec Keir (181); George Marriott (184, 185, 186, 187); Mr & Mrs Bob Milton (58, 97, 110,
111, 112, 141, 145, 149, 157); G. C. Morgan (76, 108, 206, 207); Mrs M. A. Mohamed (130, 188);
Bernard Murphy (178, 179, 180); A. Nurse (115, 121, 133, 134, 135, 152, 153, 208, 209); W.
O'Neill (66); Miss B. Parsons (88, 89, 93, 144); Tommy Parsons (148, 167); E. Peterson (164);
Miss J. M. Pippen (106, 107, 109, 114, 122, 123, 124, 125, 128, 129, 154, 155, 163); Colin Plain
(202); Reg Potter (55); H. B. Priestley (79, 80); E. C. Probert (74, 102); Mrs Kathleen Sanders (50,
103); W. Sanders (104, 105); Mrs A. J. Snelling (77, 78); John Sweeney (65); Chris Taylor
Collection (9, 10, 11, 12, 13, 14, 15, 16, 33, 34, 35, 36, 41, 42, 43, 44, 45, 69, 70, 71, 72, 81, 82,
182, 183, 214); Mrs G. M. Toogood (117, 126, 127); Bob Turner (189); Robert Virgin (131); G.
Wheaton (147, 151, 211); George White (29, 30); Stewart Williams (5); John Worrell (100, 101).

End papers: A nostalgic peep at two of the pages in The Playhouse programme for the comedy 'The Happy
Ending' featuring Violet Farebrother, which opened on Monday 10 September, 1922. Prices were Boxes
(four persons) £1.14s.0d; Orchestra Stalls 5/9d; Dress Circle 4/9d; Pit Stalls 3/6d; Upper Circle 2/4d; and
Balcony 1/-
From the Fred Jones Collection

Printed in Wales by D. Brown & Sons Ltd., Cowbridge and Bridgend, Glamorgan

Introduction

by Geoff Dart

Crockherbtown was Cardiff's oldest suburb. It was well established long before Leland described it in his *Itinerary of Wales* in 1536-9 and Speed depicted it lined with houses in his plan of 1610. How did it come about that such an ancient placename was deliberately erased almost a century ago, to be revived only in token form nearly forty years later? Perhaps this brief history may be of interest to all those, and they are many, to whom Crockherbtown is a source of curiosity and even fascination.

It was first recorded in 1348 as Crockarton, but at least one authority feels that it could have formed part of the new borough which William, Earl of Gloucester, tells us in 1171 he had made 'where my garden was outside the town of Cardiff'. The name evolved through Crockerstrete, Crokerton, Cokkerton Stret, Crockertowne, until we find the first reference to Crockherbtown in 1754. The derivation of the original form is said to be 'the home of the maker of crocks' or of a person named Croker (the latter possibly the corresponding occupational name). Dr. Donald Patterson, M.D., an authority on Cardiff placenames, says of the final form 'It is evidently the result of folk-etymology, which associated the name with "crock-herbs" or vegetables, the word being adapted to fit that view'.

In 1829 William Bird's directory describes Crockherbtown as 'now a very handsome street'; it was then about to expand on either side over the next forty years. The list of streets in Slater's directory 1885 includes a number with the district name Crockherbtown. To the south:— Tunnel Court, Hill's Street/Terrace, Frederick Street, Plymouth Street, Paradise Place, Friends' Place, Charles Street, Pembroke Terrace, Edward Terrace/Street/Place, Spring Garden Court and Station Terrace. To the north:— Park Place (developed along a former lane known earlier as Blind Lane, Dobbin Pitts Lane, Bradley's Lane), Windsor Place, Dumfries Place, St. Andrew's Crescent and Place. The same directory shows, however, that the original Crockherbtown was now more commercial than residential and was almost indistinguishable from Queen Street; the latter then terminated at the site of the East Gate (now marked out in black and red stones a little west of the Friary) and had been transformed from a narrow lane (formerly known as Running Camp and King Street) into a wide street when the Middle Row separating it from Smith Street was removed about 1863.

In December 1886 the Borough Council received a memorial (petition) from certain inhabitants of Crockherbtown and resolved 'That the name of the street between Queen Street and the Taff Vale Railway Bridge be in future called Queen Street instead of Crockherbtown and that instructions be given to the Borough Engineer to cause the said street to be renumbered forthwith'. In March 1887, however, an opposing memorial was presented to the Council by thirty property owners and residents who were 'unwilling that so well known and ancient a name, which has distinguished this as so respectable a part of Cardiff from time immemorial, should be abolished'. It was unsuccessful, as was another attempt in August 1891 by the very small margin of three votes. On the last occasion names were recorded, the Mayor, the Marquess of Bute, voting for reinstatement of the old name. As late as 1901, J. H. Matthews, the Borough Archivist, expressed to the Cardiff Naturalists' Society his forthright regret at the loss of the ancient name, referring to those who perpetrated the deed as Vandals. 'Every fourth-rate market town has its Queen Street; but Crockherbtown was distinctive, ancient and historically interesting. It did not, however, sound genteel enough for some of the shopkeepers, so it had to go. Education has made considerable strides since then. Let us hope our ''Crockherbtown'' will soon be restored.'

The Archivist's hopes were never to be realised in full. In 1923, however, Dr. Patterson suggested to the Public Works Committee that Institute Lane be renamed Crockherbtown; the Council agreed but rather spoilt the effect by retaining the word Lane. Until the opening up of the Greyfriars area between 1914 (The Friary) and 1928 (Greyfriars Road extension), this lane, in modern terms, extended only from Park Place to the exit from Andrews Arcade; it was originally a private access to the Marquess's formal 'Castle Gardens' which ran immediately to the rear of Crockherbtown and was unnamed until about 1900. Sadly, Crockherbtown Lane has never been one of Cardiff's ancient ways.

We owe a great debt to Dr. Patterson. Nevertheless, I am sure that many would agree with me that, in our more preservation conscious times, this ancient name deserves a more prominent and appropriate commemoration.

AUTHOR'S NOTE

Having reached the target I set myself in May 1980 and published ten volumes of *Cardiff Yesterday* this seems an opportune time to express my warm thanks to all who have contributed in different ways to its outstanding success. It would be impossible to list them by name in this space but a few exceptions must be made. Geoff Dart, the former County Librarian of South Glamorgan, has had a large hand in setting the high standard which has become the hallmark of the series. His knowledge of the city's history, although modestly expressed, is considerable and I am much indebted to him; Bill Barrett has also given unstinted support, willingly sharing his knowledge of old Cardiff and culling material from his wide circle of contacts; Fred Jones, as regular readers will know, has supplied many of the finest views and continues to supply me with a stream of 'gems' from his superb picture postcard collection; Chris Taylor, in addition to making available his encyclopaedic knowledge of transport (especially 'buses), has also provided some marvellous picture material; Dennis and Bill O'Neill, bless 'em, have gone to great lengths on my behalf to uncover material and photographs which have added to the interest.

As the acknowledgements show, the photographs have been drawn from literally hundreds of sources. I am deeply grateful to the donors, especially those who have taken the trouble to send their pictures to me, sometimes from overseas. The Cardiff Central Library collection has provided me with a rich seam of material and I appreciate the wholehearted support given by the County Librarian.

The books are noted for their attractiveness and this is due to the skill and expertise of my printers, D. Brown and Sons Ltd, and their staff, in particular Bob Whitaker who has personally supervised the production and Mike Pask who looks after the lay-out.

The fact that few people in Cardiff are unaware of the series is very much due to the coverage given by Geoff Rich in the pages of the *South Wales Echo* and Frank Hennessy 'on the air'.

Finally, to quash any doubts, this is NOT the end of the series. Book 11 is already in preparation and will be published in April 1985. So, please, keep sending the photographs!

1 Trem-y-Don,
Barry, CF6 8QJ,
South Glamorgan   STEWART WILLIAMS

City, Suburbs and Docks

2 The southern end of St Mary Street, 1893. The *Theatre Royal Hotel* took its name from the theatre on the opposite side of the road, afterwards named The Playhouse and later again the Prince of Wales

3 Despite competition from the lamp standard St John's Church is immediately recognisable in this 1925 view of Church Street. Oliver's original shoe shop was demolished along with Nos 1 and 2 Church Street and redeveloped as new Oliver's corner in 1976-77, and of course traffic no longer uses the street

4 An Edwardian view of Sophia Gardens Lodge which was built in 1857 and demolished by a Second World War bomb in 1941

5 Trams thread their way through Queen Street and Castle Street in this early 1929 view

DUKE STREET AND CARDIFF CASTLE

6 Interested onlookers stand in front of the trustee Savings Bank (no connection with the present-day TSB) on the corner of Duke Street and North Street (now Kingsway) as the photographer captures this rare view of old Cardiff in 1887

7 Canal bridge, Kingsway, 1910. The parapet and its twin disappeared in the widening of
Kingsway and the construction of the old Canal underpass in the mid-1970s

8 St Mary Street in 1927. Newport and Penarth 'buses wait at their respective termini on opposite
sides of the street while the man with the bucket cleans the tram points

9 St Mary Street—Quay Street—High Street junction, October 1955. Since then the *Griffin* has been demolished (May 1978) to make way for an extension to the National Westminster bank, the exterior of the TSB has been refaced, and the High Street—Quay Street corner site is now Alliance House

10 Nos 5 & 6 Working Street about to be demolished in October 1955 and eventually replaced by the first part of Mackross's new building to the left of Queen Street Arcade. No 6 was the last surviving late-18th century Working Street residence

11 The Hayes, September 1954. *Oxford Hotel*, on left, was demolished for the erection of Oxford House and Arcade *c*.1961-63; the Central Cinema, centre, and *British Volunteer*, right, went in 1966-68 for the erection of Hayes House and shops on the right side of Oxford Arcade

12 Frederick Street looking north from Bridge Street, August 1954. Weisbard's was the Mecca for generations of DIY enthusiasts. Demolished along with other properties *c*.1977 for the building of Oxford Arcade multi-storey car park

13/14 In September 1954 Hagon's and Thomas & Evans Ltd. occupied opposite corner sites in Hayes Bridge Road—Millicent Street. The T. & E. premises were demolished *c*.1958 to join the two portions of Lermon's Drapery Store. In 1982 the area was swept away for redevelopment

15   Junction of Hayes Bridge Road and Bute Terrace, July 1955. The corner buildings were demolished in 1981 followed by the *Salutation* (opened 1847) in Hayes Bridge Road in 1982

16   Junction of Hayes Bridge Road and Custom House Street, July 1955. The *Golden Cross* was saved from demolition in March 1979 when the County Council reversed its original decision after a public outcry

Cardiff Road, Llandaff.

17 Taken in 1924, the three wounded soldiers on the seats were probably from nearby Rookwood Hospital

18 An earlier view of Cardiff Road, Llandaff, looking south in 1914

7. – Cardiff Road, Llandaff

19 Ely Court, Llandaff, built for coal-owner James Harvey Insole in the second half of the last century. Acquired by the Council with the Insole Estate in 1932 and renamed Insole Court. In 1946 the name was changed again to Llandaff Court

20 Western Avenue and Llandaff College of Technology now occupy the site of Llandaff Mill here seen in 1910. The Mill House still exists on the south side of Western Avenue (WJEC offices, with extensions)

21 Surely the best picture of 'Billy the seal' to appear in this series so far. 'Billy' (actually a female grey seal) came to Victoria Park in 1912 and remained there until her death in 1939

22 General view of the Park from Victoria Park Road East with Ely Papermills in the background, *c*.1912

23 Grange Farm, Clive Street, 1913. There has been a building on this site since *c*.1200 when the monks of Margam Abbey were granted lands on the West Moors. They established the Grange here which gave its name to the district when it was built up in the 19th century

24 Albany Road looking from Richmond Road in 1927, two years after the tram poles had been removed from the centre of the road and three years before the PC on point duty was replaced by traffic lights

25/26 (*Above*) Whitchurch Post Office, Merthyr Road, in 1919 when Mr Hensch ran the PO and general shop; (*below*) general view of Merthyr Road looking south showing the location of the Post Office on the right, 1910

The Village, Whitchurch, Near Cardiff.

J. A. LEWIS

M. J. R — B. No 7717

27/28 Merthyr Road, Whitchurch, before the First World War showing (*above*) a horse 'bus making its leisurely way towards town in 1910; (*below*) a close-up of the Old Maltster's Cottages and John Lewis's draper's shop in 1908. The cottages are still there but the thatch has been replaced by traditional roofs, while the corner shop is now a two storey building

29/30 Boatmen using the Glamorganshire Canal during its 150 year life passed these white-washed houses on the stretch at Llandaff North now occupied by Gabalfa Avenue. The canal bridge and lock at College Road (*above*) was adjacent to the present Gabalfa Avenue roundabout

31 Fish pond at Roath Park, 1911. It was filled in about 1935 and grassed over

32 Old Schoolhouse at Newport Road—Ty-Mawr Road junction on Rumney Hill, 1918. St Augustine's Church is in the background. Rumney Hill was widened in 1967-68 and New Road made a 'no right turn', traffic being sent on to this junction to turn right. The small building was demolished c.1966 for this improvement

33/34 Two views of Herbert Street, Docks, in October 1955. The lower picture shows Nos 7-15 and in No 11, roughly where the van is parked, 'Peerless Jim' Driscoll lived for some years with his mother and stepfather. They later moved across the road to No 19 for a couple of years before returning to Ellen Street

35/36 Crichton Street (*above*) and Wharf Street (*below*), Docks, in October 1955. Both streets were demolished in 1979-80 for the construction of Tresillian Way, the Monument by-pass road from Bute Street to Penarth Road

37 The First World War was only months away when this busy scene was captured at Queen Alexandra Dock

38 West Dock in 1920

107. WEST DOCK, CARDIFF

QUEEN ALEXANDRA DOCK, CARDIFF.

39 A framed post-card souvenir of the entrance to Queen Alexandra Dock

40 A forest of masts in Queen Alexandra Dock and an aptly named ship in the foreground, 1920

118. QUEEN ALEXANDRA DOCK, CARDIFF

41/42 Richard England's potato wharf and warehouse dominate these Docks scenes taken in October 1955. (*Above*) the section of the Glamorganshire Canal between Bute Bridge and the northern end of West Dock. Note the passing place for barges on this narrow stretch; (*below*) on right is the West Dry Dock situated at the north-eastern corner of the West Dock. The Dock was closed in January 1964 and subsequently filled in

43/44/45 Hodge's Row acquired its name from Thomas Hodge's Dry Dock on the east bank of the Glamorganshire Canal. Although the name has survived, these original dwellings were demolished in 1955. The top two views show the south and north corners of the Row taken from Bute Street. The cottages below were the original Hodge's Row

46 Two Finnish barques, *Passat* and *Pamir*, arrived in Penarth Roads in 1949 on their last voyage from Australia. Both vessels were saved from the scrapyard by a German ship-owner. *Passat* (seen here with paddle steamer *Glen Usk* passing astern) became a training ship but was later sold to the City of Lubek for cadets' quarters

Trade and Industry

47 The façade of the *Globe Hotel* in Castle Street was new when this was taken in 1914, although its history goes back to 1792. Sadly it is no more, having been replaced by an eaterie called *Dukes*

48 Mrs Beatrice Clode, standing in the doorway (*left*) with her two children, was the licensee of the *Hastings Hotel* in Herbert Street when this was taken in 1914. She remained there during the First World War while her husband Sidney, the well-known Docks butcher, served in the Army. In the early 1930s the pub became the Irish Club. It was demolished with the rest of Newtown in 1966

49 Many a thirst was slaked in the old *Taff Vale* pub which stood on the corner of Queen Street and Paradise Place. It was first opened *c*.1868 and stayed in business until its demolition in 1977

50 Roath Park cafe in 1929 when plain teas cost 8d, fruit teas 1/4d and a pot of tea was just 4d

(opposite) James Edward Belle came from
urnsey to Cardiff and established a house re-
ring and decorating business in 1875. With
ical Victorian enterprise he also opened this
amery on the corner of Wellfield Road and
nylan Road (now occupied by Barclays Bank)
ing tea, coffee, hot chocolate, milk, cakes,
stries, etc. The founder is seated centre with
son, middle one of the three cross-legged men
straw boaters. They are the great-grandfather
d grandfather of donor K. J. Belle who still
is a decorating business. The photograph was
en in 1901 on the occasion of an outing for
employees

52   Molyneux's shop, next to the Empire in
     Queen Street, looked like this in 1906

53   Tripe was a popular meal before the First World War and Excel Products had outlets in most
parts of Cardiff

"EXCEL"

The Ready to Eat TRIPE

Try as you Buy with Salt, Pepper & Vinegar

If you are going to fry with Bacon or Onions
or Boil, do not cook longer than 10 minutes.

THE ORIGINAL TRIPE SHOPS
     35 Albany Rd, 209 Cowbridge Rd.
     92 City Road, 90 Cornwall Street

EXCEL PRODUCTS CO.

Wholesale and Retail Office:

TEL 270 760   2 Church St., Cardiff

M. M. PENNING & J. L. CUMPSTEY, PROPRIETORS.

ITS GOOD FOR YOU.

Doctors Recommend Excel Tripe.

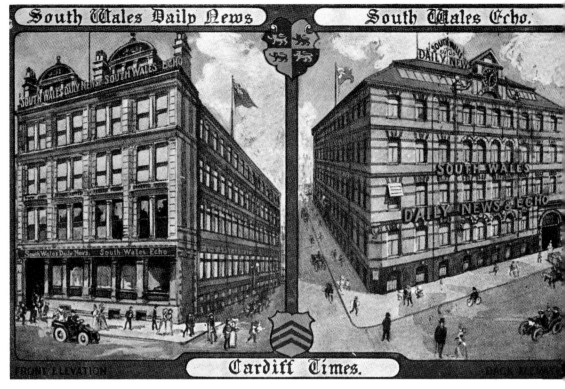

South Wales Daily News South Wales Echo.

Cardiff Times.

54 An Edwardian trade card showing the *South Wales Daily News* building in St Mary Street. The back elevation faced Westgate Street and the narrow Golate ran along the side of the building

55 *South Wales Echo* machine room and stereo staff about to start printing the special souvenir supplement on Coronation Day, 1937. Taken at the rear entrance of the old building in St Mary Street. The donor, Reg Potter, is the young apprentice holding the left-hand corner of the poster. He retired in 1982 after 50 years' service with the *Echo*

56 James's Victoria Monumental Works, 173 Cathays Terrace, backing on to Pendyris Street and opposite Gladstone Schools as it was in 1910. The business existed for 50 years. Now bushes and trees have replaced the angels and crosses

57 Quong Lee's Chinese Laundry in Crwys Road damaged during the Cardiff Seamen's Strike in 1911. One of a small group of shops opposite the old Bon Marche which were originally private houses known as Mile End Place

58 Ernie David of Penylan Farm, Caerau, on his milk round in the 1920s. Lacey's shop was at the junction of Aldsworth Road and Cowbridge Road

59 Cross Brothers staff outside the firm's St Mary Street premises about to set off on their annual outing to Brecon and Abergavenny in 1922. These premises were destroyed completely in a spectacular fire on 20 December 1935

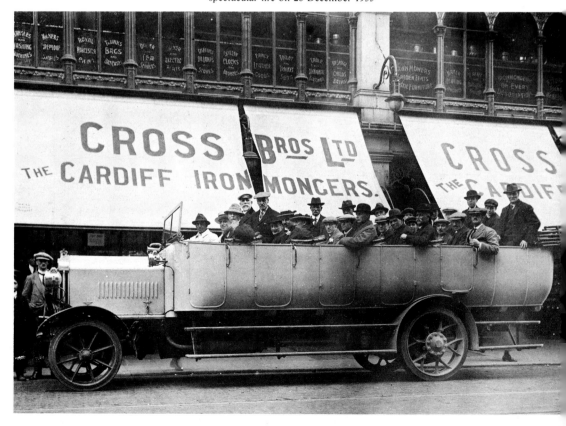

60 Cardiff shipping butchers and their wives about to set off from Cathays Park on their annual outing in 1924

61 This bull was donated to poor Cardiff families in 1912 by Charles Clode (*back, left*), the George Street shipping butcher, and fellow Docks businessmen. The presentation took place in Sophia Gardens, the beast having been transported there from Clode's farm at Dinas Powis

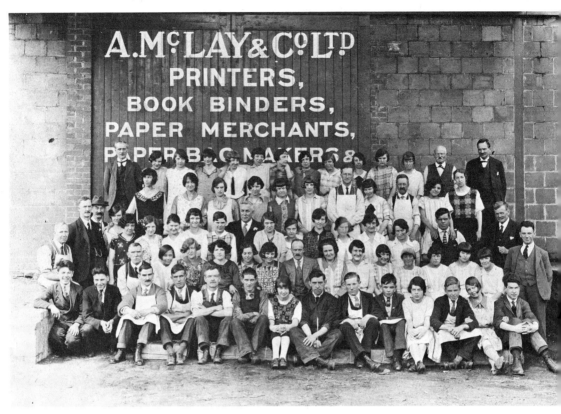

A.M^cLAY & C^oL^{TD}
PRINTERS,
BOOK BINDERS,
PAPER MERCHANTS,
PAPER BAG MAKERS &

62/63 (*Above*) Some of the staff employed by old-established Cardiff printers A. McLay & Co. Ltd, in 1928; (*below*) the binding room taken at the same time. The firm moved to purpose-built premises at Fairwater in 1921 after a fire gutted their factory in Working Street

64 Employees of Hall Lewis & Co, at the firm's Imperial Wagon Works in Freshmoor Road, Splott, before the First World War

65 Cardiff builder D. O'Neill (*centre*) with his employees on an annual outing to Wells in 1931. The firm's yard was in Crofts Street, Roath

66 Many Cardiff registered dockers are included in this group taken at a National Dock Labour Board week-end school at Porthcawl c.1953

Transport

67 Roath Railway Station in Pearl Street closed on 2 April 1917. The entrance building fronting the street has been replaced by an extension to the Roath Carlylian Club. Taken *c*.1910

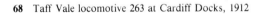

68 Taff Vale locomotive 263 at Cardiff Docks, 1912

4-001

69/70 Locomotive 5568 at Whitchurch (*above*) and approaching Rhiwbina (*below*) in June 1957. The Cardiff Docks-Queen Street to Coryton line is the only operating vestige surviving of the old Cardiff Railway. Passenger services began in March 1911 from Rhymney Railway's Parade terminus to Rhydyfelin with halts-stations at Heath (Lower Level), Birchgrove (later), Rhiwbina, Whitchurch, Coryton, Tongwynlais, Glanyllyn, Nantgarw and Upper Boat. Taken over by the GWR in 1923 and cut back to Coryton in 1931 it was due to be axed by Beeching but was reprieved and reduced to a single line with tickets issued on the train

71/72 Locomotive 5568 at Rhiwbina (*see* 69/70). Train facilities on this line were considered important enough for details to be included in prospectuses for private housing developments at Coryton, Heath Park Avenue and Rhydypennau-Cyncoed before the First World War. (*Below*) Railcar 13 at Cardiff General arriving at the westbound platform from the Newport main line on 22 October 1955. A limited number were built by the GWR in the mid 1930s and used locally on the Cardiff-Birmingham (via Stratford-upon-Avon) service. They ran just before the corresponding steam train journey and being faster were classed as businessmen's specials attracting a supplementary fare

(Opposite) **73/74** (*Above*) Women porters employed by the GWR at Cardiff General Station during the First World War; (*below*) GWR parcel van, with gas bag on top, converted from petrol during the First World War. The donor's father, Albert Probert, is the parcel boy in the centre. Taken outside the City Hall in May 1918

75 Joseph Duddridge was a proud man when he posed for this photograph in his Cardiff Railway Company uniform. He came to Cardiff in the 1870s and worked on the Docks as a labourer and coal weigher before becoming tip foreman with the railway company. He retired in 1918

76 Cardiff Corporation open-top tram at Talygarn Street—Barracks terminus in Whitchurch Road, *c.*1920. The donor's uncle, Tom Burridge, is the conductor; the driver is Tommy Littlejohn

77/78 When her brother left his job with Cardiff Corporation Transport Department to join the Army in the First World War, Alice Greenfield replaced him and worked as a tram conductress along with many other Cardiff girls. The photograph (*left*) was taken in August 1920. In August 1921 she married Albert Follett who became a well-known CCT Inspector in the 1930s

79/80 For the first half of the 20th century trams were an integral part of the city's transport system. (*Above*) Car No. 100 in Whitchurch Road working No. 1 Cathedral Road service in September 1937; (*below*) Car No. 31 at Roath Park terminus ready to set out on the No. 3 Pier Head return journey in August 1939

81/82 Arthur Ross started his road haulage business in December 1930 from an office at 112 Bute Street. He operated a fleet of twenty or so vehicles mainly on long hauls to Yorkshire, through nationalisation and denationalisation, for the next 30 years until he sold out in 1960. (*Above*) shows a newly-delivered Seddon outside the firm's Penarth Road garage; (*below*) another new delivery, an AEC Mammoth Major, at the Docks in November 1954

Religion, Education and Public Service

83 The façade and some interior features of Bethany English Baptist Chapel in Wharton Street are preserved within the premises of James Howell & Co. Built in 1821, the chapel was rebuilt in 1865 to accommodate an increase in worshippers. It declined with the movement of population to the suburbs and was eventually transferred to Rhiwbina in 1963-64

84 St Dyfrig's Church was built between 1888-1904 and demolished 1968-69 for the approach road to the new Wood Street bridge south of the old one (shown here) which was demolished in 1970

85 St Dyfrig's Clergy House (on corner with Despenser Street) and Parish Hall, Fitzhamon Embankment, 1918. The buildings are still there but ceased to have their original use with the demolition of the church

RURAL DEANERY of
CARDIFF
M? M?KENNA SAID
THERE WERE 13 CHURCHES CARDIFF
ROYAL COMMISSION ISSUED SAID
THERE 25 CHURCHES
WERE AND 13 MISSION ROOMS IN CARDIFF
IS THIS PLAYING THE GAME?

Chuch Demonstration.Cardiff 29.6.12

86 South Wales Anglicans' demonstration in Cathays Park, 1912. They were opposing disendowment provisions of the Established Church (Wales) Bill being promoted in Parliament by the Home Secretary in the Liberal Government

87 Scout Henry Little laying a foundation stone, on behalf of the Life Saving Brigade, at Swansea Street Mission Sunday School, Splott, in July 1922. Behind him stands Councillor G. Fred Evans who laid the principal stone. Moorland Road Council School is in the background

88   Choir and servers, St Mary the Virgin, Docks, in the 1950s

89   Whitsun Treat procession in North Church Street, Docks, in the 1930s

90 St Saviour's was built in 1888. This view was taken in 1925. Note the tramway clock on the extreme right

91 Members of St Saviour's Church, Splott, about to set out on their annual outing, mid 1920s

92 St Margaret's Church, Roath, in 1906 before the tower was built

93 Patronal Festival, Church of St Mary the Virgin, Docks, *c*.1924

94 Windsor Place Presbyterian Church (now United Reformed Church) Sunday School, 1916-17

95 Windsor Place Presbyterian Church Whitsun treat, 1920

96 The Duke of Kent speaking after laying the foundation stone of the Central Boys' Club, Butetown, in 1938. Construction, by Knox & Wells, was completed in 1939 but the building was taken over for war purposes and not returned to civilian use until 1947. Also in the group are the Lord Mayor (Alderman O. C. Purnell), Alderman R. G. Robinson and far left the donor's father William Edwin Iles and grandfather Edward Iles who was foreman stonemason

97 Ely Welfare Youth Club outing to the Elan Valley in 1949

98 Standard 5, Albany Road Girls' School, *c.*1910

99 Pupils of Albany Road Girls' School, 1913-14

100   After four weary years of war 'Peace Year 1919' was thankfully proclaimed on the chalked board for this Severn Road Boys' school group

101   Budding carpenters display their skills under the watchful eye of teacher in this handicraft class at Severn Road Boys' School in 1920

102 Pupils and staff of Howard Gardens Higher Grade Board School, 1889. Headmaster is J. Waugh (*centre*)

103 Pupils of Crwys Road School, 1921

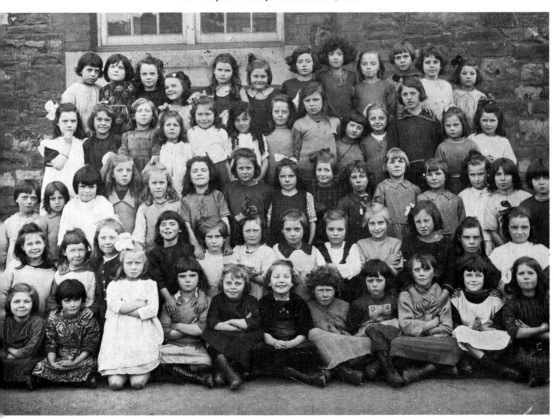

104/105 Two Tredegarville School groups. (*Above*) in 1923-24 with headmaster Mr Thomas; (*below*) taken in 1924-25

106 Marlborough Road Infants' School, 1930

107 Infants from Marlborough Road School dancing on the green in the Civic Centre during the Cardiff Schools' Annual Musical Festival in 1932

108 Standard 4, Marlborough Road School, 1934

109 St David's Day, Marlborough Road School, *c.*1936

110   Ely Council Infants, *c*.1933-34

111   Pupils of Ely Council School, 1942

112 Standard 5, Ely Council School, 1934-35

113 Windsor-Clive Infants' School, Ely, teaching staff, 1945

114 Cathays High School sports day at Heath Park, 30 June 1939

115 Pupils of Canton High School, 1945

116   Radnor Road Infants' Class 2, 1938-39

117   Pupils of Kitchener Road and St Francis Schools on a visit to Ewenny Pottery during Porthcawl Summer Camp in 1956

118/119   Two Moorland Road school groups. (*Above*) taken in 1938, and (*below*) in 1940

120 Kitchener Road Infants, 1942

121 Mr Norton's class at Ninian Park School, 1942

122　Gladstone School Choir, *c.*1953

123　Pupils of Gladstone County Secondary School pose with staff and visiting VIPs at Porthcawl Camp, *c.*1955

124/125 (*opposite*) Gladstone County Secondary Girls' School staged a Coronation Pageant 'The Queenly Tradition' on 16 July 1953 '... to look at the part women have played in the great history of our land and to express hopes that, under the leadership of our young and gracious Queen Elizabeth II, there may be even greater opportunities for women in the future'. (*Above*) from Episode One—Elizabeth I (A. E. Staniforth) at the time of the Armada; (*below*) the Finale— a salute to Queen Elizabeth II

126 'Swan Lake' performed at Kitchener Road School in 1955

127 St David's Day at Kitchener Road School, 1954. In the background is the old Railway Terrace (now demolished)

128 Headmaster R. A. Jones and staff of Waterhall County Secondary School, officially opened by George Thomas MP on 15 March 1961

129 This was Cardiff Training College, Heath Park, in the 1950s. Moved to the Cyncoed site in 1962 it became Cardiff College of Education and is currently a constituent college of South Glamorgan Institute of Higher Education

130 Pupils of the Bishop of Llandaff High School, 1964

131 Pupils and teachers of Severn Road School at Porthcawl Camp *c*.1954

LLANDAFF DIST GIRL GUIDES AT PENRICE PARK. CAMP 1931

132 More than likely some of these smiling Llandaff Guides now have grand-daughters in the Brownies and Guides

133 City Lodge laundry staff, 1916. The donor's mother, Mrs Mary Martha Nurse, is fourth from left in the front row

134/135 (*Above*) Members of St John Ambulance Brigade stationed in the Castle Mews, *c.*1948; (*right*) taking delivery of a mobile first aid unit dating from the same period

136/137 Part-time and full-time firemen and women stationed at Insole Court (renamed Llandaff Court in May 1946, *see* 19), Llandaff, at the start of the Second World War. (*Above*) Auxiliary Fire Service group taken in 1939; (*below*) a year later when it had become, along with the regular fire brigades, the National Fire Service

Sport and Entertainment

138 After showing promise in schoolboy football with Adamsdown and Cardiff Boys, local-born Ken Hollyman signed for Cardiff City from Cardiff Corries at the age of 17 in 1939. Apart from 4½ years spent in the Fleet Air Arm where he rose to the rank of Petty Officer, Ken remained at Ninian Park until 1953 making 188 first team appearances. Often described as 'the complete half back' he combined speed and ball control with one of the longest throws in football. His bubbling enthusiasm for the game made him a firm favourite with City supporters. Ken moved to Newport County in 1953 and ended his playing days with Ton Pentre. In addition to soccer he was a brilliant baseballer and played for Penylan and Wales

120. Cardiff City, 1949-50. (Back row, left to right) Arthur Lever, Stan Montgomery, Phil Joslin, Glyn Williams, Ron Stitfall, Alf Rowlands.

140 Cardiff Schools' Football League Junior XI 1957-58, winners of the Welsh Junior Schools' trophy. Captain is A. Foster (holding ball)

141 Cardiff City Colts 1945-46, Combination League champions and Welsh Youth Cup winners, with their manager Cyril Spiers (*extreme left, centre row*). Captain is Fred Sloman

142 Cardiff Corinthians, 1937-38. Regarded as the best amateur soccer club in Wales, the Corries provided a stream of talented players for Cardiff City, seven in this group—(*back row*) Les Parker (*third left*), Jack Pritchard (*fifth left*); (*middle*) Jack Steggles (*sixth left*), Billy James (*seventh left*); (*front*) Albert Stitfall (*fourth left*), Ken Hollyman (*fifth left*), Danny Lester (*eighth left*)

143 Cardiff Teachers' Training College FC, 1948-49. Captain is Leslie Jones who later played for Barry Town in the Southern League

144 St Mary's Choir Boys' soccer team in the 1920s

145 Cardiff Battalion Boys' Brigade soccer team who played Newport on the former University playing fields at Caerau in the early 1940s. The donor, Bob Milton, is seated, extreme right

146 Moorland Road School soccer team, 1943-44. Captain is Tommy Jonas. The donor, G. Green (*front left*), now lives in New Zealand

147 Radnor Road School soccer team, 1951-52 season

148 Two outstanding Roath soccer teams—the Amateurs and Argyle—with some of the cups and shield they won in the 1933-34 season

149 Cardiff sportsmen with International Sports Committee officials and the Lord Mayor and Lady Mayoress (Alderman and Mrs W. R. Wills) at the General Station prior to departing for Holland in 1946 where they took part in golf, table tennis, lawn tennis and football tournaments

150   Cardiff City Fire Service FC, 1948-49

151   St Patrick's FC, 1962-63 season

152 The lads with the football were playing on Gillard's field, later to become Sevenoaks Park. In the background of this 1915 snapshot is Lewis & Tyler's Gripoly Mills

153 Grange Nomads FC, *c.*1950

154   Cardiff Telegraphs rugby XV, 1913-14

155   Spillers' Athletic Club rugger XV, 1920-21. Captain is F. W. Pippen

156   Cardiff Supporters' 1st XV. Winners of Ninian Stuart Cup, 1927-28.
D. B. Williams (captain)

157   Cathays High School Junior Rugby XV, 1939-40. Captain is Victor Coombs

In his book *Eddie Waring on Rugby League* the author described Docks-born Billy Boston as 'one of the greatest personalities rugby has ever reared'. Billy joined Wigan in 1953 for £3000 and in the following year was selected for the Great Britain tour of Australia and New Zealand. He repaid this confidence by breaking the tour try-scoring record with 36. During his 14 years at Central Park, Billy scored 600 tries for the famous Northern club and endeared himself to supporters with his speed and skill.

158/159/160 (*Above*) Soon after joining Wigan the chairman invited Billy's Mum and Sister to watch him play at Central Park

(*Opposite, top*) Billy and Joe Erskine grew up together in the Docks and were members (*fourth and fifth from right, middle row*) of this 1948-49 Cardiff Boys' Dewar Shield winning team

(*Opposite, bottom*) Still the best of friends at the height of their sporting careers, Billy and Joe caught by the camera *c*.1960

161 Billy Boston teases a team-mate with a dummy black snake during a break from training at Woollarha Oval, Sydney, during the Great Britain team's 1954 Australian tour

162   Glantaf School netball team, season 1954-55

163   Cathays High School. End of term hockey match—staff versus pupils, 1943

164 Penylan Baseball Club 1909, winners of the South Wales Cup, also runners-up in the South
Wales & Mon. League

165 Grange Council School baseball team, undefeated Cup and League winners 1932-33-34

166 Billy Mannings (*right*) and fellow members of Splott US baseball team pose with the Dewar Shield in 1936

167 Roath United baseball team, *c*.1935

Cardiff 100 Miles Road Cycle Club was formed in 1891 and to qualify for membership applican were required to cover 100 miles in 12 hours, no mean feat on rough and ready Victorian road Seven years short of its centenary the club still holds regular Sunday runs and meets on Mondays Canton Community Centre.

168 The earliest surviving photographic record, taken in the 1901 season

169/170 Medallion presented to T. Johns in the club's foundation year to commemorate his successful completion of the road test

171 The Lord Mayor (Alderman William Grey) with officers of the 100 Miles Road Cycle Club at the 36th annual dinner on 26 January 1927

172 Cardiff '100 milers' on the steps of the YMCA in Station Terrace, *c.*1910

173 Members of the Cardiff 100 Miles Road Cycle Club marking the club's 70th anniversary with a special Sunday run starting from the *Heath Hotel* in Whitchurch Road

a brilliant career spanning the years 1928 to 1937 amateur boxer Albert Barnes had approximately 50 fights and lost only 25. A Splott boy, he joined the City Boxing Club in Hunter Street, Docks, and was trained by Charlie Davies. In his first year he won the United Services Mess Cup, displaying skills at bantam-weight which led to him winning the Welsh Amateur Championship title in 1933-34-35-36 and the British ABA in 1934-36-37. But possibly the most satisfying result for Albert was his magnificent win over Pete Scalzo in a 'Golden Gloves' tournament between American and British amateur champions held at New York's Yankee Stadium on 2 July 1935. The fight, refereed by world heavy-weight champion Gene Tunney, was watched by 48,000 fans. A measure of Albert's achievement is that Scalzo, who was battered from pillar to post, later turned professional and won the world bantam-weight crown. Another proud moment for Albert was when he represented Great Britain in the 1936 Berlin Olympic Games, attended by Adolf Hitler. Now living in retirement at Llanedeyrn, he is typically modest about his boxing days which brought great credit to himself and Cardiff.

174/175/176 (*Opposite*) Albert Barnes, reckoned by many to be the foremost amateur boxer of the day when fighting in the 1930s
(*Below, left*) Albert with the British Amateur Boxing Association Cup. He won the bantam-weight title in 1934-36-37
(*Below, right*) Identity card issued to Albert for the Berlin Olympic Games in 1936

177 Docks-born Len Horne, a member of St Mary's Boxing Club, was an outstanding amateur light-weight in the 1930s. He boxed, among others, Jack Pottinger and 'Darkie' Hughes

178 Cardiff-born Bernard Murphy (*extreme right*), well known in South Wales boxing circles as a useful middle-weight and who later became a referee and administrator, seen at Dublin Airport with Eddie Thomas (*second left*) who met Bunty Adamson in Belfast on 24 September 1953 and boxed a draw. Bernard was a first-choice sparring partner for Eddie Thomas

179 Promising young members of St David's Boxing Club, taken on 18 November 1934. 'Davo' Davies (*left*) and Bernard Murphy with their trainer, Arthur Floyd

180 Boxing personalities Bernard Murphy (*centre*) with (*left to right*) Len Harvey, Harry Carrol, Dennis Rowley and Dave Phillips aboard the 'Erskine Special' on 2 June 1958. Joe was beaten by Brian London in the 8th round in his attempt to win the Heavyweight Championship of Great Britain

1 (*opposite*) The Premier Swimming Baths and Gymnasium was located between 3 & 5 Cathedral Road near the junction with Cowbridge Road East on the site now occupied by a garage. The gymnasium was used by well-known boxers of the day, including Jimmy Wilde, for training and treatment. Taken in 1909

182/183 Cardiff's oldest surviving cinema—the Queen's in Queen Street—closed its doors for the last time on 29 October 1955 and these were taken on the last day and night. Opened in 1910 as the Picture Playhouse it later became the Cardiff Cinema Theatre before finally being named the Queen's. It was the first cinema in Cardiff to show 'talkies'—Al Jolson in The Singing Fool which ran for four months

184 The resident band at the Kennard Rooms, Richmond Road, in March 1957. (*Left to right*) Paul Wayne, Alan Wood, Gerry Evans, Bert Folon, Benny Fine, Wilf Orchard, John Collier, Norman Mills, George Marriott

185 Alto saxophonist George Marriott (Tommy's brother) was also a member of the Jack Leslie orchestra, seen here playing a gig at the *Park Hotel* in February 1950. George is in the centre in front of drummer Felix Dare

The superb musicianship of the
nmy Marriott quartette is still talked
ut by those who attended the regular
ces at the Celtic Ballroom in the Celtic
ridor (opposite the Royal Infirmary)
ng the late 1940s. With Tommy (ex-
ne right) are Tommy Pratley (piano),
ar Davies (bass) and Norman Mills
(drums)

187 Some years earlier, in 1933, Tommy
Marriott (*second from right*) was serving
his musical apprenticeship with these boys
at the Blue Horizon Club, St Mellons

188 Dockland has produced many fine musicians, among them guitarist Ray Noman (*extreme left*) and accordionist Maurice Grant (*extreme right*) seen here in relaxed mood in the early 1960s. Both played with Victor Parker in Latin American and jazz combinations

189 Resident music makers at the Bluebirds Club, Ninian Park, in the 1960s (*left to right*) Bobby Harding (transicord), Alan Giles (drums), Bob Turner (bass guitar), Jack Tarr (lead guitar)

190 Bandmaster Jim Perkins with his young St Andrew's Anglican Church fife and drum band in Cathays National School playground, 1886

191 The Lyrian Singers in 1949. This well-known Cardiff choir made numerous broadcasts and concert appearances in the inter and post-war years. Tenor Frank James (*third from right, front row*) was a member of St David's Church Choir, Ely, for many years

192 The Melingriffith Volunteer and Cadet Corps Band, 1928. Bandmaster is T. J. Powell (*seated, centre*). The dancer, Sid Grimshaw, is third from left in the second row from the back.

Memorable Events

193/194 Queen Street decorated for the Coronation Visit of King George V and Queen Mary to Cardiff in 1912; (*below*) the royal party progressing along Bute Street from the Royal Yacht to the City Hall

During the Royal visit to Cardiff on 16 March 1932 the Duchess of York was presented with a model house 'Y Bwthyn Bach', with thatched roof, as a birthday gift from the people of Wales to Princess Elizabeth. The presentation was made by the Lord Mayor (Alderman C. W. Melhuish) who described it as 'a perfect home in miniature, replete with fittings and furnishings in every way similar to an adult's home, but built to the scale of a little child of six years of age.' The house measures 22 feet long, eight feet wide, and sixteen feet high, and weighs ten tons. The architect and originator of the idea was E. C. Morgan Willmott. Furniture (including a Welsh dresser), curtains and drapery were presented by the Roath Furnishing Company.

195   The Duchess of York emerging from 'Y Bwthyn Bach'. It was her first visit to Cardiff

196 Miss L. V. Walters hands a puppy to the Duchess of York, a birthday present for Princess Elizabeth from the Welsh Terrier Society, at the model house presentation ceremony at Greyfriars Hall

197 The Duchess signing the visitors' book at City Hall watched by the Duke, The Lord Mayor (Alderman Melhuish) and Lady Mayoress (Mrs. O. Coleman)

198/199 A rare glimpse of the grand life, as enjoyed by the Bute Family in Cardiff Castle during the inter-war years, is provided by these photographs from Mrs Ann R. Jones of Heath whose grandfather Narcisse Lancien (*left*) was chef to the Marquess. Although French he was a well-known Cardiff figure and managed the *Rummer Tavern* (Hallinan's) before working for the Butes. (*Below*) Mrs Jones' father, Joseph Nicholls, also worked at the Castle as Chief Steward of the Household. He is seen here (*centre*) with two of the footmen in full ceremonial dress during Coronation Year, 1937

200 Joseph Nicholls holds an umbrella over Prime Minister Neville Chamberlain as he leaves a function at Cardiff Castle in the 1930s

201 Joseph Nicholls on hand again to serve punch to the Marquess at a meeting of the Pentyrch Hunt

202 The year is 1910 and these excited girls and boys are caught in the grip of election fever

203 Blast furnacemen at Dowlais Iron Works celebrating the first Alexandra Rose Day in 1913. It was instituted, with roses for its outward and visible sign, to mark what the Queen described as 'the 50th anniversary of my coming to this beloved country'

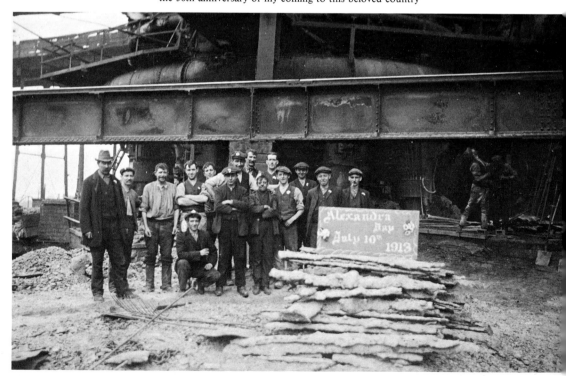

204 Cardiff Photographic Society outing, about 1935

205 Roath Carlylian Club outing to the West Country, *c*.1938

206 Silver Jubilee celebrations in Russell Street, Roath, 1935

207 'VE Day' celebrations in Russell Street, Roath, 1945

208/209 A street outing by luxury coach in the immediate post-war years was a treat and these children with their parents and grand-parents from Madras Street, Grangetown, were all smiles in happy anticipation. Taken in 1948. The street has since been demolished

210 Cardiff Flower Show, 15 July 1936. The Lord Mayor (Alderman G. Fred Evans) is third from left and seated next to him is Alderman R. G. Hill Snook who, attired in grey morning suit with buttonhole and topper to match, was a familiar figure in the streets of Cardiff for many years

211 Empire Day tea party at Fairwater Conservative Club, 1949

212 Riverside 'Holidays at Home' Carnival Queen and her attendants in Sophia Gardens, 1944

213 'VE' celebrations in Forge Place, Ely, May 1945

214 The engine room at Newport Road power station in March 1915 after a 70-ton fly-wheel coupled to one of the engines in the station burst. Fragments of it, some weighing almost a ton, were hurled through the roof and side of the building doing extensive damage

215 When John White died in September 1910 his son Sidney, the well-known showman, honoured his father's wishes and arranged a memorable funeral. The hearse was drawn by a decorated traction engine (seen here in Newport Road) and the magnificent cortege was watched by thousands of onlookers as it made its way from the family home in Tin Street to Cathays Cemetery

CENTRAL HEATING

AND

HOT WATER SUPPLY

Tel. 4456

THEATRES - - HALLS
PUBLIC INSTITUTIONS
RESIDENCES - - etc.

Call and Inspect at work
The " COOKANHEAT " RANGE
HOT WATER - COOKING
CENTRAL HEATING
FROM ONE FIRE

Hampton's Heating Co. Ltd.

18 City Road - CARDIFF

Tel. 1693,   Est. 40 years.

HILL'S FURNISHING STORES

for all kinds of

household Furniture

Note Address

North Morgan St. Canton - Cardiff

(TURN BY CANTON COLISEUM)

The following London Attractions will visit THE PLAYHOUSE only

" MONSIEUR BEAUCAIRE," with GERALD LAURENCE, MADGE COMPTON and FAY DAVIS.

MATHESON LANG in "THE BAD MAN."

"AMBROSE APPLEJOHN'S ADVENTURE."

MARIE TEMPEST.

DORAN SHAKESPEAREAN COMPANY.

IRIS HOFY in her New Play— "JILL THE GIANT KILLER."

MURRAY CARRINGTON in "MARIGOLD O' THE GARDEN."

MONDAY OCTOBER 1st
Prior production at Prince of Wales Theatre, London on October 8th, of
ELLIE NORWOOD, HILDA MOORE, and LAUDER DALE MAITLAND in

"THE RETURN OF SHERLOCK HOLMES."

'Phone 6112   'Phone 6112

100% SAVED

by buying with us a First-Class
GERMAN BABY GRAND or UPRIGHT IRON-FRAMED PIANO.

Also Pedestal Electric Gramophones
OFFICE EQUIPMENTS in Great Variety
Prices on Application   Inspection Invited
Direct Importers

FUTTER & SEGAL

35 WINDSOR PLACE, CARDIFF

After the Theatre

(FIRST HOUSE)

let's

have - something - at - the
ELECTRIC CAFE OPPOSITE
and take some cakes home with us,
made with fresh eggs and butter from their
Llan Farm - Lisvane
and cooked in Electric Ovens

Telegrams and 'Phone: 1100 Cardiff.
Glass Works - DUMBALLS ROAD.

Welsh Glass & Decorators' Supply, Ld.

PAPERHANGINGS, PAINT, OIL and COLOUR
MERCHANTS, BRITISH and FOREIGN SHEET
and PLATE GLASS, SILVERERS, BEVELL-
ERS and LEADED LIGHT MANUFACTURERS

Ask for " The Red Dragon " Pattern Book of 1923 Wall Paper Designs

MOTOR SCREENS   PLATE GLASS
PROMPTLY SUPPLIED. REPLACEMENTS.

9 & 9a Wharton Street Cardiff

Agents for 'WALPAMUR," the perfect Water Paint